Corgis as Pets

By: Lolly Brown

The Ultimate Corgi Owner's Guide

Corgi Breeding, Where to Buy, Types, Care, Cost,
Diet, Grooming, and Training all Included.

Foreword

The Corgi is a small-breed dog that has a big personality – that is what makes it such a popular pet. These little dogs are full of energy and they are highly intelligent as well! If you have ever thought about keeping a Corgi as a pet, this book may be just what you've been looking for. Within the pages of this book you will receive a wealth of information about the Corgi breed as well as tips for caring for your Corgi. By the time you finish this book you will not only know for sure whether or not the Corgi is the right dog for you, but you will also be equipped to become the best Corgi owner you can be!

Table of Contents

Introduction

The name "corgi" is given to two different breeds of dog – the Pembroke Welsh Corgi and the Cardigan Welsh Corgi. Both of these dogs are known for their short, stubby legs and their large ears. Corgis are a unique breed not only in terms of their appearance but also in their temperament. These little dogs have big personalities wrapped up in a small package. But what is it that makes these dogs so popular? There is no short answer to this question because, with Corgis, there is just so much to love.

The Corgi is more than just a pet – he is a loyal and loving companion. These dogs are active and energetic, plus they are very good with children. If you are thinking about adopting a dog or purchasing a puppy, the Corgi is definitely a great breed to consider. Before you bring a Corgi home, however, you should be a responsible dog owner and learn everything you can about this breed and how to care for it properly.

That is where this book comes in! Within the pages of this book you will learn everything you need to know in order to become the best Corgi owner you can be. Not only will you receive a wealth of information about the Corgi breed in general but you will also receive specific tips and guidelines for properly caring for your Corgi. This book includes information about creating the ideal habitat and diet for your Corgi as well as tips for breeding and showing your Corgi. You will also find in-depth health information for the breed including common health problems affecting Corgis and the treatment options available.

If you are serious about becoming a Corgi owner, turn to the next page of this book and keep reading!

Glossary of Dog Terms

AKC – American Kennel Club, the largest purebred dog registry in the United States

Almond Eye – Referring to an elongated eye shape rather than a rounded shape

Apple Head – A round-shaped skull

Balance – A show term referring to all of the parts of the dog, both moving and standing, which produce a harmonious image

Beard – Long, thick hair on the dog's underjaw

Best in Show – An award given to the only undefeated dog left standing at the end of judging

Bitch – A female dog

Bite – The position of the upper and lower teeth when the dog's jaws are closed; positions include level, undershot, scissors, or overshot

Blaze – A white stripe running down the center of the face between the eyes

Board – To house, feed, and care for a dog for a fee

Breed – A domestic race of dogs having a common gene pool and characterized appearance/function

Breed Standard – A published document describing the look, movement, and behavior of the perfect specimen of a particular breed

Buff – An off-white to gold coloring

Clip – A method of trimming the coat in some breeds

Coat – The hair covering of a dog; some breeds have two coats, and outer coat and undercoat; also known as a double coat. Examples of breeds with double coats include German Shepherd, Siberian Husky, Akita, etc.

Condition – The health of the dog as shown by its skin, coat, behavior, and general appearance

Crate – A container used to house and transport dogs; also called a cage or kennel

Crossbreed (Hybrid) – A dog having a sire and dam of two different breeds; cannot be registered with the AKC

Dam (bitch) – The female parent of a dog;

Dock – To shorten the tail of a dog by surgically removing the end part of the tail.

Double Coat – Having an outer weather-resistant coat and a soft, waterproof coat for warmth; see above.

Drop Ear – An ear in which the tip of the ear folds over and hangs down; not prick or erect

Entropion – A genetic disorder resulting in the upper or lower eyelid turning in

Fancier – A person who is especially interested in a particular breed or dog sport

Fawn – A red-yellow hue of brown

Feathering – A long fringe of hair on the ears, tail, legs, or body of a dog

Groom – To brush, trim, comb or otherwise make a dog's coat neat in appearance

Heel – To command a dog to stay close by its owner's side

Hip Dysplasia – A condition characterized by the abnormal formation of the hip joint

Inbreeding – The breeding of two closely related dogs of one breed

Kennel – A building or enclosure where dogs are kept

Litter – A group of puppies born at one time

Markings – A contrasting color or pattern on a dog's coat

Mask – Dark shading on the dog's foreface

Mate – To breed a dog and a bitch

Neuter – To castrate a male dog or spay a female dog

Pads – The tough, shock-absorbent skin on the bottom of a dog's foot

Parti-Color – A coloration of a dog's coat consisting of two or more definite, well-broken colors; one of the colors must be white

Pedigree – The written record of a dog's genealogy going back three generations or more

Pied – A coloration on a dog consisting of patches of white and another color

Prick Ear – Ear that is carried erect, usually pointed at the tip of the ear

Puppy – A dog under 12 months of age

Purebred – A dog whose sire and dam belong to the same breed and who are of unmixed descent

Saddle – Colored markings in the shape of a saddle over the back; colors may vary

Shedding – The natural process whereby old hair falls off the dog's body as it is replaced by new hair growth.

Sire – The male parent of a dog

Smooth Coat – Short hair that is close-lying

Spay – The surgery to remove a female dog's ovaries, rendering her incapable of breeding

Trim – To groom a dog's coat by plucking or clipping

Undercoat – The soft, short coat typically concealed by a longer outer coat

Wean – The process through which puppies transition from subsisting on their mother's milk to eating solid food

Whelping – The act of birthing a litter of puppies

Chapter One: Understanding Corgis

Before you decide whether or not the Corgi is the right dog breed for you, you need to learn everything you can about them. All dog breeds are unique in terms of their appearance, temperament, and housing requirements so you want to be sure that you can provide for the needs of your dog before you bring him home. In this chapter you will receive a wealth of information about the Corgi including general facts, Corgi breed history, and the different types of Corgis. By the time you finish this chapter you will have a good idea whether the Corgi is the right dog for you.

Facts About Corgis

Corgis are small dogs that have relatively long bodies in comparison to their short, stubby legs. These dogs have wide, flat skulls with long, tapered muzzles that end in a black nose. Corgis have brown, oval-shaped eyes with black rims and the ears are erect and tapered to a rounded point. Most Corgis have a short double coat, though some are born with longer fur – these dogs can only be kept as pets, since they are not acceptable for show. The most common colors for the Corgi breed include sable, fawn, red, black, and tan with white markings on the legs, chest, neck, and parts of the muzzle.

The Corgi was originally developed as a herding breed which might surprise you, since they are so small. Despite their size, Corgis can actually run very quickly and they nip at the heels of the animals they are herding to move them along. The Corgi is a very intelligent dog which makes it a highly trainable breed – in addition to herding, they also do very well as show and obedience dogs. Corgis are very loyal and eager to please their owners with whom they form very strong bonds.

Corgis are friendly by nature, though they can be a little bit wary around strangers. Proper socialization and training from a young age will help to prevent the Corgi from being suspicious of new people. Corgis do very well as family pets and they are also very good with children. This breed does need a firm and consistent hand in training, however, because they can be a little bit independent at times. Corgis have a tendency to bark which makes them good as a watchdog, though you should train your dog to stop barking on command for your own sanity.

The Corgi stands about 10 to 12 inches (25 to 30cm) tall at maturity and there is only a slight difference in size between males and females of the breed. These dogs weigh between 24 and 30 pounds (10 to 14kg) on average. Although the Corgi is a very small dog, it has a great deal of energy and needs a lot of daily exercise to work off that energy. With sufficient exercise, the Corgi can be adaptable to apartment life and they are generally calm indoors as long as they get enough mental and physical stimulation during the day.

The average lifespan for the Corgi is between 12 and 15 years and the breed is very healthy in general. Like many small dogs, however, the Corgi is prone to obesity with overfeeding and it is also prone to musculoskeletal disorders as well as eye problems. In terms of grooming, the Corgi is fairly low-maintenance. These dogs blow their coats twice a year but, in between those times, combing or brushing the coat a few times a week will be sufficient.

Summary of Corgi Facts

Pedigree: breed origins largely unknown

AKC Group: Herding Group

Types: Pembroke Welsh Corgi, Cardigan Welsh Corgi

Breed Size: small

Height: 10 to 12 inches (25 to 30cm)

Weight: 24 to 30 lbs. (10 to 14 kg)

Coat Length: short or long

Coat Texture: soft undercoat, harsh outercoat

Color: sable, fawn, red, black, and tan with white markings on the legs, chest, neck, and parts of the muzzle.

Eyes and Nose: dark brown or black

Ears: erect ears; large and tapered to a rounded point

Tail: missing or docked

Temperament: friendly, loyal, good with children, active

Strangers: may be wary around strangers, make good watchdogs

Other Dogs: generally good with other dogs if properly trained and socialized

Other Pets: strong herding instincts; may not be good with small household pets

Training: intelligent and very trainable

Exercise Needs: very active; daily walk recommended; breed is likely to develop problem behaviors without adequate mental/physical stimulation

Health Conditions: obesity, progressive retinal atrophy, glaucoma, canine degenerative myelopathy, Von Willebrand's disease

Lifespan: average 12 to 15 years

Corgi Breed History

The origins of the Corgi are somewhat difficult to trace, though it is thought that the breed originated as a Welsh cattle dog. It is unclear from the 11th century manuscript that made this reference, however, whether the dog in question was a Corgi or an ancestor of the breed. Welsh folklore suggests that the Corgi is used as a mount for fairy warriors and legend has it that Corgis were actually a gift from the fairies. In corroboration of this legend, the Corgi's markings are similar to a harness and saddle.

Another legend suggests that the Corgi was brought to Wales during the 9th and 10th century by the Vikings and Flemish weavers. As early as the 10th century, Corgis were used as herding dogs for geese, sheep, ducks, horses and cattle. In fact, this breed may be one of the oldest herding breeds in existence. Unfortunately, breeders didn't keep very good records so the history of the Corgi breed is still largely unknown.

There are actually two separate breeds of Corgi – the Pembroke Welsh Corgi and the Cardigan Welsh Corgi - though they were shown together in dog shows as early as 1925. The Corgi Club was founded in Carmathen, South Wales in 1925. Local members of the club preferred the Pembroke Welsh Corgi breed, so a separate breed club for the Cardigan Welsh Corgi was formed a year later. Both clubs engaged in selective breeding and worked to establish a standard for the breed. In 1928, both breeds were recognized by the Kennel Club as one breed – the Welsh Corgi. In 1934, however, the breeds were separated and accepted both by the Kennel Club and the AKC.

Types of Corgis

There are two distinct breeds of Corgi – the Pembroke Welsh Corgi and the Cardigan Welsh Corgi. Below you will find an overview of the differences between these two Corgi dog breeds:

Pembroke Welsh Corgi

This Corgi breed originated in Pembrokeshire, Wales and it is descendant from a line of spitz-type dogs. The Pembroke Welsh Corgi is the younger of the Corgi breeds and it is the smallest member of the Herding Group for the AKC. Pembroke Welsh Corgis are particularly famous for being the favorite breed of Queen Elizabeth II, who owned more than 30 of these dogs throughout her lifetime. These Corgis continue to be favored by British royalty. In fact, the Pembroke Welsh Corgi was rated the 25th most popular dog according to AKC registration statistics in 2011.

In comparison to the Cardigan Welsh Corgi, the Pembroke Welsh Corgi has a slightly shorter muzzle and smaller ears. This breed typically exhibits light-colored markings on either side of the withers which looks like a saddle. This breed is born with a natural short or missing tail in many cases, though in some cases puppies have their tails docked between 2 and 5 days of age.

The Pembroke Welsh Corgi has a very loving and affectionate personality and they tend to follow their owners around the house. These dogs are very smart and eager to please – in fact they are ranked as the 11th most intelligent breed according to Stanley Coren's *The Intelligence of Dogs*. Pembroke Welsh Corgis do well as herding dogs and watchdogs – they also do well as family pets since they generally get along with children. This breed has a life expectancy between 12 and 15 years and they are a "true dwarf" breed. This being the case, they may develop health problems related to their short stature and small build.

Cardigan Welsh Corgi

The Cardigan Welsh Corgi is the second of the Welsh Corgi breeds and it is known for being a very loyal family pet. These dogs are adaptable to a variety of living situations and they are highly versatile in terms of their potential for training. Cardigan Welsh Corgis are thought to have originated from the Teckel family of dogs – the same family that produced the Dachshund breed. Cardigan Welsh Corgis are among the oldest of herding breeds, having existed in Wales for more than 3,000 years. There is a great deal of folklore and legend surrounding the breed.

The Cardigan Welsh Corgi is not as popular as the Pembroke Welsh Corgi, possible because the latter was favored by British royalty for many years. This breed does, however, remain popular in the show and obedience circuits. The Cardigan Welsh Corgi has larger ears than the other Corgi breed and it has a long fox brush tail. These dogs come in a variety of colors and they often display a white blaze on the head known as the "Irish pattern". Cardigan Welsh Corgis also tend to have a longer body and darker coloring than the Pembroke Welsh Corgi.

Chapter Two: Things to Know Before Getting a Corgi

Now that you have learned the basics about the Corgi breed you should have a better idea whether or not this is the right breed for you. Still, there is more you need to learn before making your decision. In this chapter you will find a wealth of practical information about keeping Corgis as pets including licensing information, tips for keeping Corgis with other pets, and the pros and cons for this breed. You will also find an overview of the costs associated with keeping Corgis so you can determine whether you can afford one.

Do You Need a License?

Before you go out and purchase a Corgi, you need to learn whether or not it is legal for you to keep one. Licensing requirements vary from one country to another and from one state or region to another. If you are not able to find specific information about requirements for keeping dogs in your area, contact your local council for more information. Below you will find some general information about licensing requirements for dogs in the United States and in the United Kingdom.

Licensing Dogs in the U.S.

There are no federal requirements for licensing dogs in the United States – these requirements are determined at the state level. Licensing requirements vary from one state to another, but most states do require dog owners to register and license their dogs. In order to obtain a license for your dog you will probably have to provide proof that your dog has been vaccinated against rabies. Once you obtain the license you will then have to renew it each year along with your dog's rabies vaccination. Dog licenses only cost about $25 (£16.25) per year, so it is not big expense.

Even if your state or region does not require you to license your dog, it is still a good idea to do so. If your dog escapes or gets lost, having him properly identified will significantly increase the chances of you finding him. A dog license is attached to an identification number which is linked to you – if someone finds your dog, they will be able to find your contact information through the license. You can also add an ID tag to your dog's collar along with his license for good measure.

Licensing Dogs in the U.K.

Licensing requirements for dogs in the U.K. are little different from in the United States. In the U.K., it is mandatory for dog owners to license their dogs. The main difference, however, is that U.K. dog owners do not need to vaccinate their dogs against rabies because the disease has been eradicated. Dog licenses are renewed annually and they are not a significant expense.

How Many Corgis Should You Keep?

There are several important factors you need to consider when answering this question. For one thing, do you have the space and the financial ability to provide for more than one dog? Corgis are a very intelligent and active breed so they require a good deal of time and attention – think carefully before buying more than one of them. If you do have the time and money to care for a second dog, your Corgi might appreciate having another dog around to keep him company while you are away. As long as you socialize your Corgis from a young age, they shouldn't have trouble getting along with each other or with other dogs.

Do Corgis Get Along with Other Pets?

For the most part, Corgis get along with other dogs as long as they have been properly socialized from a young age – the size of the dog doesn't matter. When it comes to other pets, however, you might have a little trouble. The Corgi has strong herding instincts so your dog might develop a tendency to "herd" other pets in your household. Corgis were also used to hunt vermin, so they may be likely to chase cats and other small animals. If you raise your Corgi from a puppy with other household pets, however, you can minimize the risk for problems.

How Much Does it Cost to Keep a Corgi?

Caring for a dog is a big responsibility and it takes more than just time – it also requires money. In caring for your Corgi you will need to provide him with a healthy diet, a crate, and an assortment of toys. You will also need to make sure that he gets proper veterinary care and that he is vaccinated. These are just a few of the many costs associated with being a dog owner and you should make sure you can cover these costs before you bring a dog home. In this chapter you will find an overview of the initial costs and monthly costs associated with owning a Corgi so you can determine whether or not you are able to financially support a Corgi as a pet.

Initial Costs

The initial costs for keeping Corgis as pets include those costs you must cover before you can bring your dog home – it also includes the cost of the dog itself. Some of the initial costs you will need to cover include your Corgi's crate, food/water bowls, toys and accessories, microchipping, initial vaccinations, spay/neuter surgery and supplies for grooming and nail clipping. <u>You will find an overview of each of these costs as well as an estimate for each cost below</u>:

Purchase Price – The cost to purchase a Corgi will vary depending on the breed you choose and where you get it. It is always best to purchase from a reputable breeder because it will reduce the risk for your dog developing an inherited disease. The average cost for a Welsh Corgi puppy is between $600 and $1,000 (£540 to £900), though show-quality dogs may cost more.

Crate – Having a crate for your Corgi puppy is very important. Not only will it be used during housetraining, but it will also give your dog a space of his own where he can relax if he wants to. You'll need to purchase a fairly small crate for your Corgi puppy and you might need to buy a larger one once he reaches full size. The average cost for a puppy crate is about $30 (£19.50).

Food/Water Bowls – To feed your Corgi you'll need a food and a water bowl. The cost for these items depends on the size and quality, but you should buy something made from either stainless steel or ceramic because these materials are easier to clean. Plan to spend about $20 (£18).

Toys – To keep your Corgi puppy busy, and to keep him from chewing on your shoes or furniture, you should provide him with an assortment of toys. The cost will vary depending on the type and number of toys you buy, but budget a cost of about $50 (£32.50) to be safe.

Microchipping – There are no federal or state requirements saying that you have to have your dog microchipped, but it is a very good idea. Your dog could get out of his collar or lose his ID tag, in which case whoever finds him will be unable to identify him. A microchip is something that is implanted under your dog's skin and it carries a number that is linked to your contact information. The procedure takes just a few minutes to perform and it only costs about $30 (£19.50) in most cases.

Initial Vaccinations – During the first year of life, your Corgi puppy will need a variety of different vaccinations. If you purchase your puppy from a reputable breeder, he will probably already have had a few of these. Over the first few weeks after you bring your puppy home, however, he will need more. You should budget about $50 (£32.50) for initial vaccinations just to be prepared.

Spay/Neuter Surgery – In addition to having your Corgi puppy vaccinated, you should also have him or her spayed or neutered. The cost for this surgery will vary depending where you go and on the sex of your dog. If you go to a traditional veterinary surgeon, the cost for spay/neuter surgery could be very high but you can save money by going to a veterinary clinic. The average cost for neuter surgery is $50 to $100 (£32.50 - £65) and spay surgery costs about $100 to $200 (£65 - £130).

Supplies/Accessories – In addition to purchasing your Corgi's crate and food/water bowls, you should also purchase some grooming supplies as well as a leash and collar. The cost for these items will vary depending on the quality, but you should budget about $50 (£32.50) for these extra costs.

Initial Costs for Corgi Dogs		
Cost	**One Dog**	**Two Dogs**
Purchase Price	$600 to $1,000 (£540 - £900)	$1,200 to $2,000 (£1,080 - £1,800)
Crate	$30 (£19.50)	$60 (£39)
Food/Water Bowl	$20 (£18)	$40 (£36)
Toys	$50 (£32.50)	$100 (£65)
Microchipping	$30 (£19.50)	$60 (£39)
Vaccinations	$50 (£32.50)	$100 (£65)
Spay/Neuter	$50 to $200 (£32.50 - £130)	$100 to $400 (£65 - £260)
Accessories	$50 (£32.50)	$100 (£90)
Total	$880 to $1,430 (£792 – £1,287)	$1,760 to $2,860 (£1,584 – £2,574)

Monthly Costs

The monthly costs for keeping a Corgi as a pet include those costs which recur on a monthly basis. The most important monthly cost is food but you also need to think about things like grooming costs, license renewal, toy replacements, and veterinary exams. You will find an overview of each of these costs as well as an estimate for each cost below:

Food and Treats – The most important monthly cost you will have to cover as a dog owner is for food and treats. Because the Corgi is a fairly small dog, he will not eat as much food as a larger breed. You should plan to spend about $30 (£19.50) on a large bag of high-quality dog food which will last you at least a month. Add to this about $10 (£6.50) per month extra for treats.

Grooming Costs – The Corgi has a fairly short coat, but it is very thick and does tend to shed a lot. You should plan to have your Corgi professionally groomed about twice a year in order to keep his skin and coat in good health. If you have a longhaired Corgi, you may need to have him groomed more often. Budget about $50 and $75 (£32.50 – £68) per visit which, divided into 2 visits per year, equals a monthly grooming cost around $9 to $12.50 (£8 - £11.25) per month.

License Renewal – To purchase a license for your Corgi will generally only cost about $25 (£16.25) and you can renew it for the same price each year. License renewal cost divided over 12 months is about $2 (£1.30) per month.

Veterinary Exams – In order to keep your Corgi healthy you should take him to the veterinarian at least twice a year – keep in mind that you may need to take him more often while he is a puppy to give him the vaccines he needs. The average cost for a vet visit is about $40 (£26) so, if you have two visits per year, it averages to about $7 (£4.55) per month.

Other Costs – In addition to the cost for food, grooming, license renewal, and vet visits you will have to cover other costs on occasion. These costs may include replacements for toys, a larger collar as your puppy grows, cleaning products, and more. You should budget about $15 (£9.75) per month for extra costs.

Monthly Costs for Corgi Dogs		
Cost	**One Dog**	**Two Dogs**
Food and Treats	$40 (£36)	$80 (£72)
Grooming Costs	$9 to $12.50 (£8 - £11.25)	$18 to $25 (£16 - £22.50)
License Renewal	$2 (£1.30)	$4 (£3.60)
Veterinary Exams	$7 (£4.55)	$14 (£12.60)
Other Costs	$15 (£9.75)	$30 (£19.50)
Total	$73 to $76.5 (£65 – £69)	$146 to $153 (£131 - £138)

What are the Pros and Cons of Corgis?

Before you bring a Corgi home you should take the time to learn the pros and cons of the breed. Every dog breed is different so you need to think about the details to determine whether the Corgi is actually the right pet for you.

You will find a list of pros and cons for the Corgi dog breed listed below:

Pros for the Corgi Breed

- Small size, adaptable to apartment or condo life with proper exercise
- Very intelligent breed, typically responds well to training when started early
- Short coat is fairly easy to care for with regular brushing and combing
- Makes a good watch dog – barks when strangers or other animals enter its territory
- Generally good with other dogs and family pets
- Very loyal, forms strong bonds with family
- Friendly and easy-going breed in most cases, does well as a family pet
- Generally gets along well with children

Cons for the Corgi Breed

- Very active breed, requires a good deal of daily exercise and mental stimulation
- Can become destructive if left alone for too long
- May chase small animals and nip at the heels of children and other pets
- Barking can be a problem if not properly trained
- May be wary around strangers unless properly socialized
- Despite its short coat, sheds fairly heavy (and blows its coat twice a year)

Chapter Three: Purchasing Your Corgi

If you have decided that the Corgi is indeed the right breed for you, your next step is to learn where to get one. It might be easy to find Corgi puppies online or at a pet store, but you should put a little more thought and effort into your search than that to make sure that you get your Corgi from a reputable breeder. In this chapter you will find valuable information about where to find a Corgi breeder, how to select a reputable breeder, and how to choose a healthy puppy from a litter. You will also receive tips for puppy-proofing your home and for introducing your new Corgi puppy to your family.

Where Can You Buy Corgis?

Once you've decided that the Corgi is the right dog for you, your next step is to find one. Purchasing a Corgi might be as easy as stopping in to your local pet store since it is such a popular breed, but you should ask yourself whether this is really the best option. Many pet stores receive their puppies from puppy mills – organizations which breed dogs as quickly as they can, keeping the dogs in squalid conditions. As a result of irresponsible breeding practices, the puppies are often malnourished or suffering from health problems. The best way to make sure you get a Corgi puppy in good health is to do your research and to purchase one from a reputable Corgi breeder.

Adopting a Rescue Dog

As an alternative to purchasing a Corgi puppy, you should also consider adopting a rescue dog. Not only will you be doing your part in the war against puppy mills, but you will be providing a homeless dog with a loving home and new lease on life. There are many benefits associated with adopting a rescue dog and you might even be able to find a purebred Corgi or a Corgi puppy. Adoption is much more affordable than purchasing a purebred puppy from a breeder and the dog is likely to have already been housebroken and may also have some amount of obedience training as well.

If you are thinking about adopting a Corgi, consider one of the Corgi rescues below:

U.S. Corgi Recues

Pembroke Corgi Rescue.
<http://pembrokecorgirescue.webs.com/>

For Paws Corgi Rescue.
<http://www.forpaws.org/>

Pet's Second Chance Rescue.
<http://www.petssecondchance.org/corgi-info>

Pembroke Welsh Corgi Rescue Network.
<http://pwcca.org/about-pembrokes/pwc-rescue-network>

Cardigan Welsh Corgi National Rescue Trust.
<http://cardiganrescue.org/>

Sunshine Corgi Rescue, Inc.
<http://www.sunshinecorgirescue.org/how-to-adopt/>

U.K. Corgi Rescues

Welsh Corgi Rescue Service.
<http://www.welshcorgirescue.co.uk/>

Kennel Club Welsh Corgi Breed Rescue Index.
<http://www.thekennelclub.org.uk/services/public/findaresc
ue/Default.aspx?breed=5145>

How to Choose a Reputable Corgi Breeder

When you purchase a Corgi puppy you are making a 12 to 15-year commitment. This being the case, you want to make sure that you put the right amount of thought into the decision. To make sure that you bring home a Corgi puppy who is healthy and well-bred, you should take the time to find a reputable breeder. <u>Below you will find a list of steps to help you find a Corgi breeder</u>:

1. Ask around at veterinary offices, groomers, and pet stores for referrals to Corgi breeders and assemble as much information as you can about each one.

2. Visit the website for each breeder (if they have one) and check to see if the breeder is registered with a national

or local breed club (like the AKC or Kennel Club).

3. Contact each breeder individually and ask them questions about their knowledge of the Corgi breed as well as their breeding experience.

4. Ask specific questions about the breeder's program and the dogs used to produce the puppies – you should also ask what the breeder does to prevent the passing of congenital conditions to the puppies.

5. Remove the breeders from your list who do not seem to be knowledgeable about the breed or if they seem to be just hobby breeders looking to make a buck.

6. Eliminate breeders from your list who refuse to answer your questions or who do not seem genuinely concerned for the wellbeing of their puppies.

7. Schedule a visit with several breeders and ask for a tour of the facilities – check to make sure they are clean and that the dogs look healthy.

8. Narrow down your list of breeders and make your selection – you should also ask about the breeder's preferences for putting down a deposit on a puppy.

9. Place your deposit to reserve a puppy – in the next section you will receive tips for choosing a puppy from a litter.

U.S. Corgi Breeders

Misty Ridge Pembroke Welsh Corgis.
<http://www.mistyridgecorgis.com/>

Hagaren Cardigan Welsh Corgis.
<https://hagarencardigans.wordpress.com/>

Wendt Worth Champion Bred Pembroke Welsh Corgis.
<http://www.wendtworthcorgis.com/>

Pembroke Welsh Corgi Club of America, Inc. Directory.
<http://pwcca.org/about-the-pwcca/membership-directory>

Cardigan Welsh Corgi Club of America Breeder Directory.
<http://cardigancorgis.com/BreederDirectory.asp>

U.K. Corgi Breeders

Liebhund Cardigan Corgis.
<http://www.liebehund.co.uk/>

Vuedor Corgis.
<http://www.vuedorcorgis.co.uk/>

Balletcor Pembroke Welsh Corgis.
<http://www.pembrokecorgi.co.uk/>

Kennel Club Assured Breeders Directory.
<http://www.thekennelclub.org.uk/services/public/acbr/Defa
ult.aspx?breed=Welsh+Corgi+(Pembroke)>

Tips for Selecting a Healthy Corgi Puppy

After you've narrowed down your options and selected a breeder comes the fun part – choosing your puppy! Do not simply pick the first Corgi puppy that comes waddling up to you – you should be just as careful in your selection of a puppy as you were in choosing a breeder. Below you will find a list of steps to follow to make sure you pick a healthy Corgi puppy from the litter:

1. Take a moment to speak to the breeder about the puppies – make sure that they are the proper age to be separated from the mother (at least 8 weeks of age).

2. Step back and observe the puppies as a litter – watch how they interact with each other and make sure they display normal puppy behavior.

3. Look for signs that the puppies are nervous or fearful of people – they shouldn't run away or hide when you approach them.

4. Make sure the puppies are active and playful – they should not be lethargic or laying around.

5. Approach the puppies to see if they display a healthy curiosity about you – a little timidity is fine, but they shouldn't be terrified of you.

6. Let the puppies come up to you and give them a minute to sniff around and lick your hands.

7. Pick up one puppy at a time and see how it reacts to being handled.

8. Examine the puppies for obvious signs of ill health – there shouldn't be any signs of discharge from the nose or mouth, no swelling or discoloration on the body, they should have a healthy coat, etc.

9. If possible, watch the puppies being fed to make sure they have a healthy appetite and no problems eating solid food.

10. Look around the facility for red flags – signs of diarrhea or dirty conditions can be an indication that the puppies might not be in good health.

11. Play with the puppies to get a feel for their individual temperaments then pick the one that suits you best.

Note: A reputable breeder won't let you take home a puppy that is younger than 8 weeks. Some states even have laws which prohibit the sale of puppies under 8 weeks of age. It is important to wait until the puppy is fully weaned and eating solid food before you bring him home.

Puppy-Proofing Your Home

Before you bring your Corgi puppy home you need to make sure that your home is ready. This requires more than just setting up your puppy's crate and food bowl – you also need to go around your house and take steps to improve safety for your puppy. Below you will find a list of steps to follow in puppy-proofing your home:

- Place all of your food in tightly lidded containers and store them in the cupboard or pantry.

- Make sure your trashcan has a tight-fitting lid and store your garbage out of your puppy's reach.

- Pick up small objects from the floor and put them away – this includes things like toys, rubber bands, pieces of string, etc.

- Store all of your medications (prescription and over-the-counter) safely in a medicine cabinet.

- Keep all of your cleaning supplies stored away where your puppy can't get into them – this includes supplies kept in the garage.

- Remove any toxic houseplants from your home or move your plants so they are well out of your puppy's reach.

- Check to make sure none of the plants on your property are toxic to dogs – if they are, remove them or fence them off so your puppy can't get into them.

- Cover any open bodies of water that could pose a drowning hazard for your puppy – this includes toilets, sinks, ponds, pools, and more.

- Make sure all of the outlets in your home are protected by plastic covers.

- Tie up the cords for your blinds as well as electric cords so your puppy can't chew on them.

These are just a few of the many things you should do to keep your puppy safe at home. After going through the items on this list, walk around your house and view things from your puppy's eyes – remove anything that he might be tempted to chew on or play with that could be harmful.

Chapter Four: Caring for Your New Corgi

The Corgi makes a wonderful pet largely due to his friendly and loving personality, but these dogs are also very adaptable to different types of living situations. In this chapter you will find some basic information about cultivating a happy and healthy home life for your Corgi. You will find tips for setting up your Corgi's crate as well as valuable information about making sure your Corgi's exercise needs are met.

Ideal Habitat Requirements for Corgis

One of the things that makes the Corgi so popular is its small size. These dogs are very active by nature, but they can adapt to small living spaces like apartments and condos. The main thing your Corgi needs in terms of its habitat is plenty of love and affection from his human companions and adequate daily exercise. The Corgi is a very loyal and loving breed that bonds closely with family so you should make an effort to spend some quality time with your Corgi each and every day. If your Corgi doesn't get enough attention he may be more likely to develop problem behaviors like chewing or excessive barking.

In addition to playing with your Corgi and spending time with him every day, you also need to make sure that his needs for exercise are met. The Corgi was developed as a herding breed so these dogs are naturally very active. Though these dogs can be kept in smaller living quarters, they still require a lot of daily exercise to work off their energy. A long daily walk or run plus some active play time will be very important for your Corgi. You should also make sure your Corgi gets plenty of mental stimulation from interactive toys and games.

Supplies and Equipment to Have on Hand

In order to care for your Corgi properly you will need to have certain things on hand. Most importantly, your Corgi needs a crate or carrier to sleep in (you will also use it for housetraining) as well as food and water dishes and other accessories. <u>You will find an overview of the required supplies and accessories to have on hand</u>:

- Crate or carrier
- Blanket or dog bed
- Food and water dishes
- Toys (assortment)
- Collar, leash and harness
- Grooming supplies

Crate or Carrier – Having a crate or carrier for your Corgi serves two important functions. First, it will give your Corgi a place to sleep as well as a place to retire to if he needs some time to himself. Second, it will play an important role in housebreaking your Corgi. Choose a carrier that is just large enough for your Corgi to comfortably stand up, turn around, sit, and lie down in. You may need to purchase one crate for your Corgi as a puppy and upgrade it once he reaches full size.

Blanket or Dog Bed – To make your Corgi's crate more comfortable you will need to line it with a soft blanket or pet bed. Choose something that is comfortable but also easy to wash. While your Corgi is being housebroken, you might even want to get something waterproof.

Food/Water Dishes – Food and water dishes for dogs come in all shapes and sizes but you should choose a set that suits your dog's needs. Corgis are a small-breed dog, so don't choose anything too large. You should also think about sanitation – stainless steel and ceramic bowls do not harbor bacteria like plastic can and they are easy to clean.

Toys – To keep your Corgi occupied you will need to provide him with an assortment of toys. Making sure your Corgi has plenty of toys will keep him from chewing on your shoes and it will give you something to use in playing with him.

Collar, Leash and Harness – Having a collar for your Corgi is incredibly important because you will need to attach your dog's license and ID tag to it. Choose a collar appropriate for your Corgi's size – it should fit well without being too tight or too loose. Choose a leash that won't weigh your Corgi down during walks and consider investing in a harness as well. Harnesses offer improved control over your dog's movements and they take the pressure off your dog's neck and throat.

Grooming Supplies – In order to keep your Corgi's skin and coat in good health you'll need to brush and comb him several times a week. Have a wire pin brush on hand as well as wide-toothed comb. You may also want to buy an undercoat rake to help remove dead hairs from your Corgi's coat before he sheds them all over your furniture.

Once you have assembled all of these items you can use them to create a living space for your Corgi. You will find tips for setting up your Corgi's crate in the next section of this book.

Setting Up Your Corgi's Crate

Once you have assembled all the necessary supplies you can set up your Corgi's crate. It is a good idea to set up your dog's crate in an area that gives him some space to call his own. Choose a room that isn't in the center of the action, but it shouldn't be too secluded either. The ideal location will offer enough space for you to set up a puppy play pen in addition to your dog's crate and supplies.

Setting up a puppy playpen will mean that you can confine your Corgi puppy at times when you cannot watch him but he'll have more freedom to move around than he would in his crate. Place the crate in the play pen or build a wall around the area surrounding the crate to create your own pen. Make sure you place your puppy's food and water bowls nearby as well as a box of his toys.

Chapter Five: Meeting Your Corgi's Nutritional Needs

One of the best things you can do to keep your Corgi healthy is to provide him with a high-quality, balanced diet. The food you offer your Corgi will have a direct impact on his health and wellness, so choosing the right diet is very important. In this chapter you will learn the basics about the nutritional needs for your Corgi as well as some special considerations for feeding this type of dog. You will also receive tips for choosing a commercial dog food brand and info about foods you should never feed your dog.

The Nutritional Needs of Dogs

Like all living things, dogs require a balance of protein, fats, and carbohydrates in their diet as well as certain vitamins and minerals. When you think about the proper diet for dogs, you probably already know that meat plays an important role. This is true, but you should not overlook the other nutrients your dog needs. Below you will find an overview of the nutrients essential to your dog's diet and where they come from:

Protein – Protein is made up of amino acids and it is incredibly important for the growth and development of your Corgi's issues, organs, and cells. Dogs require animal-based proteins like fresh meat and meat meals because it provides them with the essential amino acids they cannot produce on their own. Plant-based proteins are less biologically valuable for your dog, though they are not essentially harmful.

Fat – Fat is the most highly concentrated source of energy available to your dog and it is particularly important for small-breed dogs like the Corgi since they have such high energy needs. Like protein, fats should come from animal-based sources like chicken fat and fish oil instead of plant-based sources like flaxseed or canola oil. You should make sure your Corgi gets a balance of omega-3 and omega-6 fatty acids to ensure proper skin and coat health.

Carbohydrate – Dogs do not have specific requirements for carbohydrate in their diet, but carbohydrates do provide dietary fiber as well as valuable vitamins and minerals. Your dog should get his carbohydrate from whole grains like brown rice or oatmeal – these are the most digestible sources. Gluten-free and grain-free alternatives like sweet potato and tapioca are also good choices. Just be sure to avoid low-quality carbohydrates made from corn and soy ingredients because they provide very little nutritional value – dog food companies just use them to add bulk to their products without increasing cost or nutritional value.

Vitamins – Your dog needs to get certain vitamins from his diet because his body cannot produce them on his own. The most important vitamins for dogs are vitamin D, vitamin A, vitamin C and vitamin E.

Minerals – Because minerals are inorganic compounds, your dog's body cannot synthesize them – they must come from his diet. The most important minerals for dogs include copper, calcium, phosphorus, potassium, sodium, and iron.

Water – In addition to macronutrients and micronutrients, your Corgi also needs plenty of fresh water on a daily basis. About 70% of your dog's bodyweight is made up of water so, if he doesn't drink enough water during the day, it can have a serious negative impact on his health.

Now that you understand the nutrients your dog needs in his diet you can learn a bit more about his specific energy needs. Small-breed dogs like the Corgi have much higher energy needs than large-breed dogs because they have very fast metabolisms. A large-breed dog like a 110-pound Akita might need a total daily calorie intake of 2,500 calories, but that only amounts to about 23 calories per pound of bodyweight. A 22-pound Corgi, on the other hand, needs about 750 calories a day but that equates to about 34 calories per pound of bodyweight.

The actual number of calories your Corgi needs on a daily basis will vary according to his age, sex and weight. You can actually calculate your Corgi's calorie needs using the following formula: **RER = 30 (weight in kg) + 70**. In this formula, RER stands for Resting Energy Requirement – the amount of calories your dog's body will burn just to maintain metabolic function. Once you've calculated this number you can then multiply it by a certain factor according to his age and activity level. <u>You will find a chart of these factors below</u>:

Type of Dog	Daily Calorie Needs
Weight Loss	1.0 x RER
Normal Adult (neutered)	1.6 x RER
Normal Adult (intact)	1.8 x RER
Lightly Active Adult	2.0 x RER
Moderately Active Adult	3.0 x RER
Pregnant (first 42 days)	1.8 x RER
Pregnant (last 21 days)	3.0 x RER
Lactating Female	4.8 x RER
Puppy (2 to 4 months)	3.0 x RER
Puppy (4 to 12 months)	2.0 x RER

To give you an example, consider a neutered male Corgi that is 3 years old and weighs 25 pounds. To calculate this Corgi's RER, you would multiply the number 25 by 2.2 to determine his weight in kilograms (about 11.3 kg) – then you simply multiply that number by 30 and add 70. This gives you a total RER of 409. You would then use the chart above and multiply that number by a factor of 1.6 (for a neutered adult male) and get a total daily calorie need of about 654 calories. Because the Corgi is a fairly active breed, however, you would probably want to use either the lightly active adult or moderately active adult factor.

How to Select a Healthy Dog Food Brand

Now that you have a basic understanding of your Corgi's nutritional and calorie needs you can think about shopping for a high-quality dog food. Your Corgi should be fed a high-quality commercial dog food that is specially formulated for small-breed dogs. Many dog food companies offer formulas for small-breed puppies as well as small-breed adults, so choose the formula that is right for your Corgi, depending on his age.

Shopping for dog food can be difficult because there are so many different options to choose from. In order to separate the high-quality foods from the low-quality foods, you need to learn how to read a dog food label. When comparing dog foods, the first thing you want to look for is the AAFCO statement of nutritional adequacy – this will tell you that the product meets the basic nutritional needs of dogs. AAFCO is the American Association of Feed Control Officials and the statement of nutritional adequacy will look something like this:

"[Product Name] is formulated to meet the nutritional levels established by the AAFCO Dog Food nutrient profiles for [Life Stage]."

After you've determined that the product is approved by AAFCO, you can then take a more detailed look at the ingredients list. Remember, protein is the most important nutritional consideration for dogs so you should look for a high-quality source of protein (or two) at the top of the ingredients list. Ingredients lists for dog foods are assembled in descending order by volume – this means that the ingredients at the top of the list are present in the highest quantities. So, if a product lists something like deboned chicken or fresh turkey as the first ingredient, you can assume that the product is a good source of protein.

When perusing dog food labels, you are likely to come across meat meals like chicken meal or salmon meal. The word "meal" might turn you off, but it is actually a very good ingredient to have in a dog food. Fresh meats contain up to 80% water so, by the time the product is cooked, the actual volume of the meat is much lower than it was originally. Meat meals have already been cooked down to a moisture level around 10% so they are actually a much more concentrated source of protein than fresh meat.

In addition to high-quality proteins, you should also look for digestible carbohydrates like whole grains and fresh vegetables. Things like brown rice and oatmeal are valuable additions to a commercial dog food while products like corn gluten meal or wheat flour are not. Gluten-free and grain-free carbohydrates like sweet potato and tapioca starch are also good ingredients if you are looking for a product that is free from gluten and grains. Just try to avoid byproduct meals as well as corn and soy ingredients. When it comes to fats, you should look for animal-based fats like chicken fat and salmon oil – these are much more biologically valuable to your dog than plant-based fats like canola oil or flaxseed. You should look for a blend of both omega-3 and omega-6 fatty acids as well.

Not only do you need to be mindful of the ingredients included in your dog's food, but you should also be mindful of things that are NOT included. Avoid products made with artificial preservatives like BHT and BHA. You also want to look for products free from artificial flavors, colors and dyes. If your Corgi suffers from food allergies, consider a Limited Ingredient Diet (LID) which is made with a novel source of protein that won't trigger his allergies. Novel sources of protein might include things like bison, venison, or even kangaroo meat.

Tips for Feeding Your Corgi

When it comes to feeding your Corgi, you may be wondering how much food is too much. The Corgi is one of the many breeds prone to obesity and once your dog becomes obese it can be difficult for him to lose weight. Your best bet is to follow the feeding recommendations on the dog food package as a starting place. Follow the feeding recommendations for a few weeks and keep an eye on your Corgi's weight. If he starts to gain weight, you may need to cut back on his portions a little bit. If your dog loses weight or doesn't appear to have as much energy as he used to, you may need to feed him a little bit more.

Another important thing to consider in feeding your Corgi is how many times you should feed him per day. Small-breed dogs like the Corgi have very fast metabolisms so it is generally a good idea to divide his daily portion into three or four smaller meals rather than feeding him one or two large meals per day. You also need to remember that Corgis have small stomachs, so they cannot eat a lot of food at once. This is why small-breed dog foods are so nutrient dense – they need to meet your dog's nutritional needs in a smaller amount.

While your Corgi is still a puppy, you might be able to feed him freely instead of rationing his meals. Just keep in mind that your Corgi puppy will reach his maximum size more quickly than a large-breed dog, at which point you should switch him to an adult dog food formula. Monitor your Corgi puppy's growth and once he reaches about 80% of his maximum expected size, make the switch. Your veterinarian should be able to help you estimate your Corgi's maximum size.

Dangerous Foods to Avoid

It might be tempting to give in to your dog when he is begging at the table, but certain "people foods" can actually be toxic for your dog. As a general rule, you should never feed your dog anything unless you are 100% sure that it is safe. <u>Below you will find a list of foods that can be toxic to dogs and should therefore be avoided</u>:

- Alcohol
- Apple seeds
- Avocado
- Cherry pits
- Chocolate
- Coffee
- Garlic
- Grapes/raisins
- Hops
- Macadamia nuts
- Mold
- Mushrooms
- Mustard seeds
- Onions/leeks
- Peach pits
- Potato leaves/stems
- Rhubarb leaves
- Tea
- Tomato leaves/stems
- Walnuts
- Xylitol
- Yeast dough

If your Corgi eats any of these foods, contact the Pet Poison Control hotline right away at (888) 426 – 4435.

Chapter Six: Training Your Corgi

Perhaps your most important job as a dog owner is training your Corgi. The Corgi is a very intelligent breed which means that he responds well to training, though you should maintain a firm and consistent hand to prevent this breed from developing small dog syndrome. Corgis are very trainable but you do need to start this breed with training and socialization early for the best results. In this chapter you will receive information about socializing your Corgi. You will also find information about various dog training methods and specific tips for housebreaking your Corgi and getting started with obedience training.

Socializing Your New Corgi Puppy

The first few weeks of your Corgi puppy's life are incredibly important. Not only is this when you will establish a bond with him, but it is also when he is the most impressionable. Socialization is essential for puppies when they are young because the experiences they have during this impressionable period will determine who they are as an adult. If your puppy isn't properly socialized, he might turn into a shy and timid adult dog who responds to new people and unfamiliar situations with fear or uncertainty instead of normal curiosity.

Socializing your new Corgi puppy is not difficult – all you have to do is spend time with him and introduce him to new things. Socialization can be as simple as taking your puppy on a walk in new places, introducing him to other puppies, introducing him to new people, and playing different games. Your puppy will absorb new experiences like a sponge so, the more you expose him to, the better off he will be. Just keep an eye on your puppy to make sure isn't becoming overwhelmed during the process.

Overview of Popular Training Methods

In addition to socializing your new Corgi puppy you should also begin training as soon as possible. Corgis are very intelligent and eager to learn, so starting with training early will increase your chances of having a well-behaved and obedient adult dog. When it comes to dog training, there are many different methods to choose from. Some of the most popular methods include positive reinforcement, punishment, alpha dog, and clicker training. You will find an overview of each training method below:

Positive Reinforcement – This method of training hinges on your dog's natural desire to please. In essence, you train your dog to repeat desired behaviors by rewarding him for doing them. For example, if you want your dog to sit when you give him the "Sit" command, teach him what the command means and then reward him each time he responds to the command appropriately. Positive reinforcement training is one of the most popular and effective dog training methods.

Punishment – This type of training is almost the opposite of positive reinforcement training – rather than rewarding your dog for performing desired behaviors, you punish him for performing unwanted behaviors. The punishment used doesn't have to be violent or cruel – it can be as simple as withdrawing your attention to teach your dog to stop whining. In short, you give the dog the opposite of what he wants to curb the negative behavior in question. This type of training is more effective as a method for curbing negative behaviors than for teaching positive behaviors.

Alpha Dog – This type of training was made popular by the Dog Whisperer, Cesar Milan. Milan believes that dogs are natural pack animals and that dog owners must establish themselves as the leader of the dog's "pack". This means that you must make your dog submissive to you so he will submit to your will. Alpha dog training involves things like never letting the dog walk through the door before you, or waiting to feed your dog until after you have eaten. This training method works for some people but it is not endorsed by the ASPCA and other animal rights groups.

Clicker Training – This type of training is a version of positive reinforcement training and it is highly popular. The key to success with positive reinforcement training lies in helping your dog to identify the desired behavior – that is where the clicker comes in. You go through the normal process of training, giving your dog a command and guiding him to perform the desired behavior. Then, as soon as he displays the behavior you click the clicker and immediately issue a reward – this helps your dog to learn more quickly which behavior it is that you desire. You should only use the clicker during the first few repetitions of a training sequence until your dog learns what the desired behavior is – you don't want him to become dependent on the clicker to perform that behavior.

Housebreaking Your Corgi Puppy

After socialization, housetraining is probably one of your most important tasks as a dog owner. While your Corgi puppy is still young, he will not be physically capable of holding his bladder or bowel movements. Making sure to take your puppy outside very frequently (as often as once an hour) will help to reduce the frequency of accidents until your puppy is old enough for housetraining. The most effective method for housetraining a puppy is crate training. You'll find a step-by-step guide for this housetraining method below:

1. Follow the guidelines provided earlier in this book to choose a crate for your puppy and set it up as directed.

2. Get your puppy used to the crate by tossing treats into it and feeding him his meals in the crate.

3. Eventually your puppy should be comfortable enough with the crate to take naps in it with the door open.

4. Start closing the door to the crate while your puppy is inside and leave him there for a few minutes.

5. Gradually increase the length of the confinement until your puppy can remain calm in the crate for at least 30 minutes.

6. Start housetraining by selecting a certain area of the yard where you want your puppy to do his business.

7. Take your puppy to that area each time you take him outside and give him a verbal command like "go pee".

8. When your puppy does his business in the area, praise him excitedly and offer a reward to reinforce the behavior.

9. Keep your puppy in the same room as you at all times when you are at home and supervise him closely.

10. Take your puppy outside every hour or two, especially after naps and within 30 minutes after a meal.

11. If your puppy does not do his business when you take him out, take him right back inside and try again in 30 minutes.

12. When you are not at home or unable to watch your puppy, confine him to the crate – avoid leaving any food or water which might increase his risk for having an accident.

13. Be sure not to leave your puppy in the crate for longer than he is physically capable of holding his bladder and bowels.

14. Gradually increase the length of the time your puppy spends in the crate until he can make it overnight.

15. Always take your puppy outside immediately after releasing him from the crate and before you put him in it.

Chapter Seven: Grooming Your Corgi

Most Corgis have short, double coats that require little more than regular brushing and grooming. Some Corgis, however, have longer coats that are a little more difficult to maintain. No matter what kind of coat your Corgi has, it is your job to groom it properly so it remains in good health. In this chapter you will learn the basics about grooming your Corgi – this includes brushing and bathing your dog as well as trimming his nails, cleaning his ears, and brushing his teeth.

Recommended Tools to Have on Hand

If your Corgi has a short coat, you will not need to do very much maintenance – brushing a few times a week and bathing as needed should be sufficient. If you have longhaired Corgi, however, the task of grooming can be a little more challenging. No matter what kind of coat your Corgi has, it is essential that you have the right tools on hand to complete the job. <u>You will find a list of several recommended grooming tools and supplies below</u>:

- Wire pin brush
- Metal comb
- Undercoat rake
- Small, sharp scissors
- Dog-friendly shampoo
- Nail clippers
- Dog-friendly ear cleaning solution
- Dog toothbrush
- Dog-friendly toothpaste

As long as you have these supplies on hand you should be able to do most of your Corgi's grooming yourself at home. Still, you might want to have your Corgi professionally groomed twice a year for good measure.

Tips for Bathing and Grooming Corgis

Now that you know what tools and supplies you need to have on hand for grooming your Corgi you are ready to learn the process. You should brush your Corgi's coat as often as possible – at least once a day is recommended to keep your dog's skin and coat in good healthy while also reducing shedding. If you only have time to groom your Corgi a few times a week, that is okay because his short fur doesn't tend to tangle much.

The first step in grooming your Corgi is to go over his body with a metal comb. Start at the back of the head and work your way down the dog's neck and back, brushing in the direction of hair growth. Move on to the dog's sides and comb the fur down each leg. Once you've gone over your Corgi with a comb to remove tangles you can do it again with the wire pin brush to collect loose and dead hairs. If your Corgi is a particularly high shedder (most Corgis blow their coats twice a year) you may also want to use an undercoat rake to remove dead hairs from the Corgi's undercoat before they can be shed.

After you've gone over your Corgi with the comb and brush he is ready for bathing. Remember, the Corgi doesn't need to be bathed frequently – you should only do it when he really needs it. If you bathe your dog too frequently it could cause his skin and coat to dry out. When you do bathe your dog, be sure to use dog-friendly shampoo that will be gentle on his skin. <u>Below you will find a step-by-step guide for bathing your Corgi</u>:

1. Place a non-slip mat or towel on the bottom of your tub then fill it with a few inches of warm water (not hot water).

2. Put your Corgi in the tub and use a handheld sprayer or a container to wet down his coat as thoroughly as possible. (Keep in mind that the Corgi has a double coat, so it may take some effort to ensure that the water penetrates all the way through).

3. Apply a small amount of your dog-friendly shampoo to your hand then work it into your Corgi's coat, forming a thick soapy lather.

4. Work the soap through the hair on your dog's neck, back, legs, chest and tail – avoid getting his ears, eyes, and nose wet.

5. Thoroughly rinse away the soap using clean water until all traces have been removed.

6. Use a damp washcloth to carefully clean the fur on your dog's head and face, if necessary, keeping the eyes and ears dry.

7. Towel-dry your Corgi using a large fluffy towel until you've removed as much moisture from his coat as possible.

8. If it is cold out and your Corgi is shivering, finish drying his coat using a hairdryer on the low heat setting – otherwise, you may be able to let your Corgi air dry.

The most important thing to remember when bathing your Corgi is that you must keep his ears dry. Wet ears are a breeding ground for bacteria and infection. Fortunately, the Corgi has erect ears which ensures plenty of airflow to the ear canal, but there is always a risk for ear infections so be very careful.

Other Grooming Tasks

In addition to brushing and bathing your Corgi, you also need to engage in some other grooming tasks including trimming your dog's nails, cleaning his ears, and brushing his teeth. <u>You will find an overview of each of these grooming tasks below</u>:

Trimming Your Corgi's Nails

When it comes to trimming your dog's nails, you need to be very careful. Each of your dog's nails contains a quick – the blood vessel that supplies blood to the nail. If you cut the nail too short and sever this blood vessel it could not only hurt your dog, but it could cause profuse bleeding as well. The best way to prevent this from happening is to make sure you have the right tool and to learn the proper nail trimming procedure before you do it yourself. Ask your vet or a professional groomer to show you how to trim your dog's nails and then, when you do it yourself, be sure to only trim away the sharp tip.

Cleaning Your Corgi's Ears

Cleaning your Corgi's ears isn't a difficult task, but he might not like it. A dog's ears are a breeding ground for bacteria so, if you do not keep them clean, your dog may have an increased risk for recurrent ear infections. To clean your dog's ears, add a few drops of a dog-safe ear cleaning solution to your dog's ear canal. Then, massage the outside of your Corgi's ears by hand to spread the solution. Next, use clean cotton balls to clean away any buildup inside your dog's ears (as well as excess cleaning solution). Then, just let your Corgi's ears air dry.

Brushing Your Corgi's Teeth

The idea of brushing your dog's teeth might sound silly but it is actually a very important part of grooming. Periodontal (dental) disease is incredibly common among pets and it can actually lead to some serious health problems including tooth loss, heart disease, and organ damage. To brush your Corgi's teeth, place a small amount of dog-friendly toothpaste on a dog toothbrush. Brush just a few of your dog's teeth at a time until he gets used to the process. Be sure to reward your dog after brushing his teeth so he learns that good behavior earns him a treat. This will make things much easier for you in the long run.

Chapter Eight: Breeding Your Corgi

     Breeding your dog is not a decision that you should make lightly because it is a big responsibility. Not only will you be responsible for caring for a litter of puppies until they are old enough to send to new homes, but you will also have to care for a pregnant dog. If you are thinking about breeding your Corgi to make some extra money, think again – hobby breeders are lucky if they come out even after breeding and selling the puppies. There are also many potential complications that could affect your Corgi during breeding, so think carefully before you breed.

Basic Dog Breeding Information

When it comes to dog breeding, no matter what breed you choose, you need to be absolutely sure of your decision before you begin. Breeding dogs of any breed is a huge responsibility and it can take a financial toll on your family as well. Unfortunately, many dog owners out there think that breeding their dogs is a good way to make some extra money. The reality is, however, that by the time you pay for healthcare costs for your pregnant female and a litter of puppies (not to mention food and housing for all of them), you will be lucky to come out even.

If you do not plan to breed your Corgi, the ASPCA recommends having him or her neutered or spayed before 6 months of age. For female dogs, they should be spayed before their first heat. In smaller breeds, the first heat may occur before 6 months of age, so have your female Corgi spayed as early as it is safe to do so. Keep in mind that spaying and neutering dogs before 6 months of age can significantly reduce their risk for certain types of cancer and other serious diseases.

If you are absolutely sure that you want to breed your Corgi, you need to learn everything you can about the breeding process for dogs before you begin. The most important thing you need to learn about is the estrus cycle.

This is the cycle also known as "heat" through which female dogs go about twice a year. The cycle lasts for 14 to 21 days on average and it occurs about every 6 months once it becomes regular – it can take a few years for a dog to establish a regular cycle.

When your female Corgi goes into heat, there will be several signs you can look for. The first sign is swelling of the vulva – your dog may also excrete a bloody discharge at the start of the cycle, though many dogs do not develop this until the 7th day of the cycle. As your Corgi's cycle progresses, the discharge will become lighter in color until it is pink and watery by the 10th day of the cycle. In addition to this discharge, many female dogs start to urinate more frequently during their cycle – they might also develop urine marking behavior to attract male dogs.

A male dog can smell a female in heat from very great distances, so you need to be very careful to keep your female Corgi indoors while she is in heat. When you take her outside, be sure to keep her on a leash and supervise her closely. Never take a female dog in heat to the dog park or to another location where intact male dogs may be present. If you intend to breed your Corgi, you want to avoid any accidental mating.

When the discharge from your dog's vulva becomes light in color and watery, this is likely when she will be the most fertile and when she will begin to ovulate – this generally happens around day 11 to 15 of the cycle. It is during this time that you want to introduce her to the male dog to make an attempt at breeding. If you introduce the dogs too early in the female's cycle she might not be receptive to him. If she isn't, just wait another day or two before trying again. Your Corgi is technically capable of conceiving at any point during her cycle because the sperm from the male dog can survive in the reproductive tract for as long as 5 days.

Tips for Breeding Your Corgi

Now that you know the basics about breeding dogs you can learn the specifics about Corgis. The Corgi has a gestation period lasting about 63 days (or 9 weeks). The gestation period is the period of time following conception during which the puppies develop in the mother's uterus. The average litter size for the Corgi breed is between 6 and 8 puppies. Keep in mind that new mothers will often have smaller litters – the next few litters will generally be larger before the litter size starts to taper off again.

Again, the Corgi gestation period lasts about 63 days but you won't be able to tell that your Corgi is pregnant right away. By the 25th day of pregnancy it is safe to perform an ultrasound on the pregnant dog. Around day 28 to 32, your veterinarian will be able to feel the puppies by palpating the mother's uterus. After 6 weeks, it is safe to use x-rays to confirm pregnancy and litter size.

To increase your chances of a successful breeding, you need to keep track of your Corgi's estrus cycle. Once your female reaches the point of ovulation, you can introduce her to the male dog and let nature take its course. Breeding behavior varies slightly from one breed to another, but you can expect the male dog to mount the female from behind (as long as she is receptive). If the breeding is successful, conception will occur and the gestation period will begin.

While the puppies are developing inside your female Corgi's uterus, you need to take special care to make sure the female is properly nourished. You do not need to make changes to your dog's diet until the fourth or fifth week of pregnancy. At that point you should slightly increase her daily rations in an amount proportionate to her weight gain. It is generally best to offer your dog free feeding because she will know how much she needs to eat. Make sure your dog's diet is high in protein and fat to support the development of her puppies – calcium is also very important.

Raising Healthy Corgi Puppies

By the eighth week of pregnancy you should start preparing yourself and your dog for the whelping. This is the time when you should set up a whelping box where your female dog can comfortably give birth to her puppies. Place the box in a quiet, dim area and line it with newspapers and old towels for comfort. The closer it gets to the whelping, the more time your dog will spend in the whelping box, preparing it for her litter.

During the last week of your Corgi's pregnancy you should start taking her internal temperature at least once per day – this is the greatest indicator of impending labor. The normal body temperature for a dog is about 100°F to 102°F (37.7°C to 38.8°C). When your dog's body temperature drops, you can expect contractions to begin within 24 hours or so. Prior to labor, your dog's body temperature may drop as low as 98°F (36.6°C) – if it gets any lower, contact your veterinarian.

Once your Corgi starts going into labor you can expect her to show some obvious signs of discomfort. Your dog might start pacing restlessly, panting, and switching positions. The early stages of labor can often last for several hours and contractions may occur as often as 10 minutes apart. If your Corgi has contractions for more than 2 hours without any of the puppies being born, contact your veterinarian immediately. Once your dog starts giving birth, the puppies will arrive about every thirty minutes following ten to thirty minutes of straining.

After each puppy is born, the Corgi will lick the puppy clean. This also helps to stimulate the puppy to start breathing on his own. Once all of the puppies have been born, the mother will expel the rest of the placenta (the afterbirth) and then let the puppies start nursing. It is essential that the puppies begin nursing within one hour of being born because this is when they will receive the colostrum from the mother. Colostrum is the first milk produced and it contains a variety of nutrients as well as antibodies to protect the pups until their own immune systems have time to develop. In addition to making sure that the puppies are feeding, you should also make sure that the mother eats soon after whelping.

The average weight for a Corgi puppy at birth is about 10 ounces (285g). Most Corgi puppies are born tail-less or with a natural bob – if they are not, many Corgi breeders have the tails bobbed between 3 and 5 days of age. Corgi puppies are born blind, with their eyes and ears closed, so they will be completely dependent on the mother for several weeks. Around week 3, the puppies will open their eyes and their ears will become erect sometime after. As the puppies grow, they will start to become increasingly active and the will grow very quickly as long as they are properly fed by the mother.

At six weeks of age is the time you should begin weaning the puppies by offering them small amounts of puppy food soaked in water or broth. The puppies might sample small bits of solid food even while they are still nursing and the mother will general wean the puppies by week 8, with or without your help. If you plan to sell the puppies, be sure not to send them home unless they are fully weaned at least 8 weeks old. You should also take steps to start socializing the puppies from an early age to make sure they turn into well-adjusted adults.

Chapter Nine: Showing Your Corgi

The Corgi is a wonderful dog to keep as a pet but this breed has the potential to be so much more than that. These dogs are highly intelligent and trainable which makes them a great choice as a show dog. In order to show your Corgi, however, you have to make sure that he meets the requirements for the breed standard and you need to learn the basics about showing dogs. In this chapter you will receive information about the breed standard for both Corgi breeds and you will find general information about preparing your dog for show.

Corgi Breed Standard

Because there are two different Corgi breeds, each one has its own breed standard. <u>Below you will find an overview of the standard for both the Pembroke Welsh Corgi and the Cardigan Welsh Corgi as published by the American Kennel Club</u>:

Pembroke Welsh Corgi Standard

General Appearance – The Pembroke Welsh Corgi is low-set with a sturdy build without being heavy-boned. The expression is intelligent, not shy or vicious. The dog should have a smooth, free gait.

Temperament – The dog is bold but kind, neither shy nor viscous. Shyness is considered a disqualification.

Size, Proportion, Substance – The height should be 10 to 12 inches and the weight not exceeding 30 pounds for dogs, 28 pounds for bitches. The proportions should be long and low, the substance not light-boned or heavy-boned.

Head, Skull, Muzzle, and Ears – The head is foxy in shape with an intelligent, interested expression. The skull is wide and flat between the ears with a moderate stop and slightly rounded cheeks. The eyes are oval and brown, in harmony with the coat color. The ears are erect and firm, medium in size and tapering to a rounded point.

Legs and Body – The neck is fairly long, the topline firm and level. The rib cage is well sprug, the chest deep, and the tail docked short. The legs are short with forearms turned slightly inward. The hindquarters exhibit ample bone with well-muscled thighs.

Coat and Color – The coat is medium-length with a short, weather-resistant undercoat and longer, coarse outer coat. The coat lies flat with the hair slightly longer on the underparts and back of the forelegs. Straight coat is preferable, though some waviness is permissible. The coat should be in self colors of red, sable, fawn, black and tan, with or without white markings. White body color and red or dark markings are faults. The Corgi should be shown in natural condition with no trimming except on the feet.

Cardigan Welsh Corgi Standard

General Appearance – The Cardigan Welsh Corgi is low-set with a deep chest and moderately heavy one. The silhouette is long in proportion to the height with a low-set, fox brush tail. The overall appearance is intelligent and powerful.

Temperament – The dog is even-tempered and affectionate, neither shy nor viscous. The dog is also loyal and adaptable in nature.

Size, Proportion, Substance – The height should be 10 ½ to 12 ½ inches and the weight between 30 and 38 pounds for dogs, 25 to 34 pounds for bitches. The proportions should be balanced with a length/height ratio of 1.8:1.

Head, Skull, Muzzle, and Ears – The head is refined and in balance with the rest of the dog. The skull is moderately wide and flat between the ears and the muzzle rounded but not blunt. The eyes are medium to large and dark, in harmony with the coat color. The ears are large and prominent, slightly rounded at the tip.

Legs and Body – The neck is moderately long and well developed, the body long and strong. The tail is set fairly low, never curled over the back. The chest is moderately broad, tapering to a deep brisket, with shoulders sloping downward. The forearms are curved and the hindquarters well-muscled and strong.

Coat and Color – The coat is medium-length and dense with a short, insulating undercoat and a harsh outercoat. The coat lies flat with the hair slightly longer on the underparts and back of the forelegs. Straight coat is preferable, though some waviness is permissible. The Corgi should be shown in natural condition with no trimming except on the feet. The coat may be in all shades of red, sable and brindle as well as black or blue merle. Any white on the head should not predominate and it shouldn't surround the eyes.

Preparing Your Corgi for Show

Once you've determined that your Corgi is a good representation of the breed standard, then you can think about entering him in a dog show. Dog shows occur all year-round in many different locations so check the AKC or Kennel Club website for shows in your area. Remember, the rules for each show will be different so make sure to do your research so that you and your Corgi are properly prepared for the show. <u>Below you will find a list of some general recommendations to follow during show prep</u>:

- Make sure that your Corgi has been housetrained completely before registering him for a show.

- Ensure that your dog is properly socialized to be in an environment with many other dogs and people.

- Make sure that your Corgi has had at least basic obedience training – he needs to respond to your commands and follow your lead in the show ring.

- Research the requirements for the individual show and make sure your Corgi meets them before you register.

- Take your Corgi to the vet to ensure that he is healthy enough for show and that he is caught up on his vaccinations – the bordatella vaccine is especially important since he'll be around a lot of other dogs.

- Pack a bag of supplies for things that you and your Corgi are likely to need at the show.

- Have your Corgi groomed the week of the show and take steps to make sure his coat stays in good condition.

Below you will find a list of helpful things to include in your dog show supply pack:

- Registration information
- Dog crate or exercise pen
- Grooming table and grooming supplies
- Food and treats
- Food and water bowls
- Trash bags
- Medication (if needed)
- Change of clothes
- Food/water for self
- Paper towels or rags
- Toys for the dog

Chapter Ten: Keeping Your Corgi Healthy

As you have already learned, the key to keeping your Corgi happy and healthy is to feed him a balanced diet and to make sure that he gets enough exercise on a daily basis. Even if you provide these things, however, the Corgi is prone to developing certain health problems. In some cases, there is nothing you can do to prevent these problems but the speed with which you respond to them can determine whether or not your dog makes a full recovery. In this chapter you will learn the basics about common conditions affecting the Corgi breed and you will receive some tips for vaccinating your dog to prevent illness.

Common Health Problems Affecting Corgis

Feeding your Corgi a healthy diet is one of the most important things you can do to make sure he stays well. Even if you do gives your Corgi the best diet available, however, he might still develop an illness now and then. The key to making sure that your dog recovers quickly and fully is to identify the disease as early as possible and to get the proper treatment. In this chapter you will find a list of common conditions affecting the Corgi breed including their cause, symptoms, and treatment options so you will know what to do if your Corgi gets sick.

Common Conditions Affecting Corgis:

- Degenerative Myelopathy
- Epilepsy
- Glaucoma
- Hip Dysplasia
- Hypothyroidism
- Intervertebral Disk Disease
- Progressive Retinal Atrophy
- Von Willebrand's Disease

Degenerative Myelopathy

Degenerative myelopathy is a progressive disease which affects the spinal cord in older dogs. This disease typically manifests between 8 and 14 years of age, beginning with loss of coordination in the dog's hind limbs. At first the dog will wobble when walking or drag the feet – this might occur in one limb or both. As the disease progresses, the limbs become increasingly weak and the dog might have difficulty standing. Eventually, the weakness will worsen to the point of paralysis and the dog will be unable to walk.

This disease is caused by degeneration of the white matter in the dog's spinal cord. This degeneration may or may not be caused by the mutation of a certain gene. In order to diagnose your Corgi with degenerative myelopathy your veterinarian will perform tests to rule out other causes of the weakness. These tests may include MRI, myelography, and biopsy of the spinach cord. In many cases, however, the diagnosis cannot be completely confirmed except with an autopsy (necropsy). Unfortunately, there are no treatments available to slow or stop the progression of degenerative myelopathy. The best treatment is to manage the dog's symptoms and to keep him as comfortable as possible. The use of harnesses and carts is common for dogs who have lost the use of their hind limbs.

Epilepsy

Epilepsy is a seizure disorder that may manifest in several different ways. In most cases, seizures are preceded by a focal onset phase during which the dog may appear dazed or frightened. During the seizure, the dog typically falls to its side and becomes stiff, salivating profusely and paddling with all four limbs. Canine seizures generally last for 30 to 90 seconds and they most commonly occur while the dog is resting or asleep.

There are two types of canine epilepsy – primary and secondary. Primary epilepsy is also called true epilepsy or idiopathic epilepsy – this type of epilepsy involves seizure with an unknown cause. This condition usually presents between 6 months and 5 years of age and it may have a genetic link. Secondary epilepsy is a condition in which the cause of the seizures can be determined. The most common causes for secondary epilepsy include degenerative disease, developmental problems, toxins/poisoning, infections, metabolic disorders, nutritional deficiencies, and trauma.

Veterinarians use information about the age of onset and pattern of the seizures to make a diagnosis. Treatment options for canine epilepsy may involve anticonvulsant medications and monitoring of the dog's health and weight.

Glaucoma

The Corgi breed is prone to several eye-related conditions including glaucoma. Glaucoma is a very common condition in which the fluid inside the dog's eye builds and creates intraocular pressure that is too high. When the pressure inside the eye increases, it can lead to damage of the internal structures within the eye. If this condition is not treated promptly, it can lead to permanent loss of vision or total blindness for the dog.

There are two types of glaucoma – primary and secondary. Primary glaucoma involves physical or physiological traits that increase the dog's risk for glaucoma – this is usually determined by genetics. An example of a trait that might increase the dog's risk for glaucoma is small drainage pores that lead to accumulated fluid within the eye. Secondary glaucoma occurs when the glaucoma is caused by another condition such as a penetrating wound to the eye or other causes for inflammation.

Glaucoma can sometimes be difficult to diagnose in the early stages, but common signs include dilated pupil, cloudiness of the eye, and rubbing the eye. If you notice any of these symptoms, seek immediate treatment. Treatment options include topical solutions to reduce pressure, increase drainage, and to provide pain relief.

Hip Dysplasia

Hip dysplasia is a very common musculoskeletal problem among dogs. In a normal hip, the head of the femur (thigh bone) sits snugly within the groove of the hip joint and it rotates freely within the grove as the dog moves. Hip dysplasia occurs when the femoral head becomes separated from the hip joint – this is called subluxation. This could occur as a result of abnormal joint structure or laxity in the muscles and ligaments supporting the joint.

This condition can present in puppies as young as 5 months of age or in older dogs. The most common symptoms of hip dysplasia include pain or discomfort, limping, hopping, or unwillingness to move. As the condition progresses, the dog's pain will increase and he may develop osteoarthritis. The dog may begin to lose muscle tone and might even become completely lame in the affected joint.

Genetics are the largest risk factor for hip dysplasia, though nutrition and exercise are factors as well. Diagnosis for hip dysplasia is made through a combination of clinical signs, physical exam, and x-rays. Surgical treatments for hip dysplasia are very common and generally highly effective. Medical treatments may also be helpful to reduce osteoarthritis and to manage pain.

Hypothyroidism

This condition is very common in dogs and it can produce a wide variety of symptoms. Hypothyroidism occurs when the thyroid gland fails to produce enough thyroid hormone – this often leads to weigh loss as well as hair and skin problems. Fortunately, this condition is easy to diagnose with a blood test that checks the dog's levels of certain thyroid hormones like T4.

The thyroid is a gland located in your dog's neck close to the voice box, or larynx. The activity of the thyroid is regulated by the pituitary gland in the brain which produces thyroid stimulating hormone (TSH). Hypothyroidism occurs when the thyroid produces insufficient thyroid hormone – this is most often caused by a destruction of the thyroid gland. This is often associated with other diseases like cancer or atrophy of the thyroid tissue. The use of certain medications can affect the thyroid gland as well.

Hypothyroidism is most commonly diagnosed in dogs between 4 and 10 years of age. The main symptoms of this disease include lethargy, hair loss, weight gain, excessive shedding, hyperpigmentation of skin, slow heartrate, high blood cholesterol and anemia. Treatment usually involves daily treatment with synthetic thyroid hormone.

Intervertebral Disk Disease

Intervertebral disk disease (IVDD) is another musculoskeletal issue common in Corgis. This condition causes a wide variety of different symptoms ranging from mild pain to completely paralysis – it can also mimic the presentation of other musculoskeletal problems which can delay diagnosis. IVDD can occur in any breed, though it is more common in certain breeds including the Corgi.

The symptoms of IVDD are highly variable and may include neck pain or stiffness, back pain or stiffness, abdominal tenderness, arched back, lameness, sensitivity to touch, stilted gait, reluctance to rise, loss of coordination, tremors, collapse, and paralysis. These symptoms most commonly present after strenuous activity of physical trauma. The most common cause of this condition is related to a disorder of cartilage formation called chondrodystrophy and it usually presents in dogs aged 3 to 6 years old.

There are both medical and surgical treatment options available for intervertebral disk disease. Medical treatments may involve corticosteroids or non-steroidal anti-inflammatories aimed to treat pain and control inflammation. Surgical treatments may help to decompress the spinal cord or to inject enzymes to help stabilize the affected disks.

Progressive Retinal Atrophy

Another eye problem known to affect the Corgi breed is progressive retinal atrophy, or PRA. This condition affects more than 100 different breeds and it is generally an inherited condition passed on through the genes. PRA affects the retina of the eye, the part that receives light and converts it into electrical nerve signals that the brain interprets as vision. Dogs with PRA typically experience arrested retinal development (called retina dysplasia) or early degeneration of the photoreceptors in the eye. Dogs with retinal dysplasia usually develop symptoms within 2 months and are often blind by 1 year.

The signs of PRA vary according to the rate of progression. This disease is not painful and it doesn't affect the outward appearance of the eye. In most cases, dog owners notice a change in the dog's willingness to go down stairs, or to go down a dark hallway – PRA causes night blindness which can progress to total blindness. Unfortunately, there is no treatment or cure for progressive retinal atrophy and no way to slow the progression of the disease. Most dogs with PRA eventually become blind. Fortunately, dogs often adapt well to blindness as long as their environment remains stable.

Von Willebrand's Disease

Von Willebrand's disease (or vWD) is a disease of the blood that affects certain dog breeds more than others. This disease is caused a deficiency of von Willebrand Factor (vWF) in the dog's blood. Von Willebrand Factor is a type of adhesive glycoprotein found in the blood which is required for normal platelet binding, or clotting. Lack of vWF can lead to excessive bleeding following even a minor injury. It may also cause nosebleeds, bloody urine, bloody stool, bleeding gums, and vaginal bleeding (in females). It can also cause bruising and anemia.

This disease is an inherited condition caused by genetic mutations that affect the synthesis, release and stability of vWF. In order to diagnose vWD, your veterinarian will perform a physical exam as well as a medical history. Blood count and blood chemical profiles will also be obtained along with a urinalysis and electrolyte panel. The best treatment for von Willebrand's Disease is transfusion with fresh plasma and fresh blood to increase the supply of vWF in the blood. Fortunately, this condition can be managed in mild to moderate cases. Dogs with more severe vWD may require additional transfusions for surgery and supportive care may be required following spontaneous bleeding episodes.

Preventing Illness with Vaccinations

While some diseases affecting the Corgi breed are not preventable (this mainly applies to congenital conditions), others are. Having your Corgi vaccinated is the best way to protect him from common canine diseases like distemper and parvovirus. It is important to have your puppy vaccinated at an early age and to follow your vet's recommendations for annual booster shots. <u>To give you an idea what kind of vaccinations your puppy will need, consult the vaccination schedule below</u>:

Vaccination Schedule for Dogs			
Vaccine	**Doses**	**Age**	**Booster**
Rabies	1	12 weeks	annual
Distemper	3	6-16 weeks	3 years
Parvovirus	3	6-16 weeks	3 years
Adenovirus	3	6-16 weeks	3 years
Parainfluenza	3	6 weeks, 12-14 weeks	3 years
Bordatella	1	6 weeks	annual
Lyme Disease	2	9, 13-14 weeks	annual
Leptospirosis	2	12 and 16 weeks	annual
Canine Influenza	2	6-8, 8-12 weeks	annual

Your Corgi will not necessarily need all of the vaccinations on this list – some of them are only given to dogs that live in areas of high risk. You should also remember that if you purchase your puppy from a breeder, he may have already been given some vaccines. Check with the breeder and ask for a health history of your puppy and then share it with your veterinarian to make sure your puppy gets the right vaccinations.

Corgi Care Sheet

In reading this book you have received a wealth of information regarding the Corgi as a pet. This information should be sufficient for you to make an educated decision regarding whether or not the Corgi is the right breed for you. If it is and you decide to purchase a Corgi, this book will be a valuable reference for you but you might not always have time to skim through the whole book to find answers to your questions. So, in this chapter, you will find a Corgi care sheet that summarizes all of the most important facts and information about the Corgi breed so you can find it quickly and easily.

1.) Basic Corgi Information

Pedigree: breed origins largely unknown

AKC Group: Herding Group

Types: Pembroke Welsh Corgi, Cardigan Welsh Corgi

Breed Size: small

Height: 10 to 12 inches (25 to 30cm)

Weight: 24 to 30 lbs. (10 to 14 kg)

Coat Length: short or long

Coat Texture: soft undercoat, harsh outercoat

Color: sable, fawn, red, black, and tan with white markings on the legs, chest, neck, and parts of the muzzle.

Eyes and Nose: dark brown or black

Ears: erect ears; large and tapered to a rounded point

Tail: missing or docked

Temperament: friendly, loyal, good with children, active

Strangers: may be wary around strangers, make good watchdogs

Other Dogs: generally good with other dogs if properly trained and socialized

Other Pets: strong herding instincts; may not be good with small household pets

Training: intelligent and very trainable

Exercise Needs: very active; daily walk recommended; breed is likely to develop problem behaviors without adequate mental/physical stimulation

Health Conditions: obesity, progressive retinal atrophy, glaucoma, canine degenerative myelopathy, Von Willebrand's disease

Lifespan: average 12 to 15 years

2.) Habitat Requirements

Recommended Accessories: crate, dog bed, food/water dishes, toys, collar, leash, harness, grooming supplies

Collar and Harness: sized by weight

Grooming Supplies: wire pin brush, wide toothed comb, undercoat rake

Grooming Frequency: brush several times a week; professional grooming 2 to 3 times a year

Energy Level: fairly high; bred for herding

Exercise Requirements: at least 30 minutes per day plus active playtime

Crate: highly recommended

Crate Size: just large enough for dog to lie down and turn around comfortably

Crate Extras: lined with blanket or plush pet bed

Food/Water: stainless steel or ceramic bowls, clean daily

Toys: start with an assortment, see what the dog likes; include some mentally stimulating toys

Exercise Ideas: play games to give your dog extra exercise during the day; train your dog for various dog sports

3.) Nutritional Needs

Nutritional Needs: water, protein, carbohydrate, fats, vitamins, minerals

RER: 30 (weight in kg) + 70

Calorie Needs: varies by age, weight, and activity level; RER modified with activity level

Amount to Feed (puppy): feed freely but consult recommendations on the package

Amount to Feed (adult): consult recommendations on the package; calculated by weight

Important Ingredients: fresh animal protein (chicken, beef, lamb, turkey, eggs), digestible carbohydrates (rice, oats, barley), animal fats

Important Minerals: calcium, phosphorus, potassium, magnesium, iron, copper and manganese

Important Vitamins: Vitamin A, Vitamin A, Vitamin B-12, Vitamin D, Vitamin C

Look For: AAFCO statement of nutritional adequacy; protein at top of ingredients list; no artificial flavors, dyes, preservatives

4.) Breeding Information

Age of First Heat: around 6 months (or earlier)

Heat (Estrus) Cycle: 14 to 21 days

Frequency: twice a year, every 6 to 7 months

Greatest Fertility: 11 to 15 days into the cycle

Gestation Period: 59 to 63 days

Pregnancy Detection: possible after 21 days, best to wait 28 days before exam

Feeding Pregnant Dogs: maintain normal diet until week 5 or 6 then slightly increase rations

Signs of Labor: body temperature drops below normal 100° to 102°F (37.7° to 38.8°C), may be as low as 98°F (36.6°C); dog begins nesting in a dark, quiet place

Contractions: period of 10 minutes in waves of 3 to 5 followed by a period of rest

Whelping: puppies are born in 1/2 hour increments following 10 to 30 minutes of forceful straining

Puppies: born with eyes and ears closed; eyes open at 3 weeks, teeth develop at 10 weeks

Litter Size: average 6 to 8 puppies

Size at Birth: about 10 ounces

Weaning: start offering puppy food soaked in water at 6 weeks; fully weaned by 8 weeks

Socialization: start as early as possible to prevent puppies from being nervous as an adult

Index

brushing   10, 30, 70, 71, 72, 75, 76

C

cage   4, 23
calories   53, 55
cancer   78, 99
Canine Influenza   104
carbohydrates   51, 52, 57, 109
Cardigan Welsh Corgi   4, 6, 1, 13, 15, 16, 17, 34, 38, 87, 89, 123, 124
care   3
care sheet   105
carrier   46
castrate   5
cause   73, 75, 94, 96, 100, 102
Cavalier King Charles Spaniel   11, 106
chewing   25, 45, 47
children   1, 10, 11, 16, 30, 31, 106
clicker training   64
clinic   26
clipping   23
coat   4, 5, 6, 7, 9, 10, 11, 28, 30, 31, 40, 48, 52, 70, 71, 72, 73, 74, 88, 89, 90, 92,
       106
collar   20, 25, 26, 29, 47, 107
color   5, 6, 11, 106
coloration   6
coloring   4
colors   6, 9, 17, 58, 88
colostrum   84
comb   5, 48, 71, 72, 107
command   5
complications   77
conception   81, 82
condition   5
contractions   83
coordination   95, 100

F

G

H

I

K

L

M

N

O

P

Q

R

S

T

Photo Credits

Cover Page Photo By FatFairfax via Wikimedia Commons, <https://commons.wikimedia.org/wiki/File:Welsh_Corgi_Ca rdigan_Licking.jpg

Page 1 Photo By Frei Sein via Wikimedia Commons, <https://commons.wikimedia.org/wiki/File:Pembroke_Welsh _Corgi_600.jpg>

Page 8 Photo By Pmuths1956 via Wikimedia Commons, <https://en.wikipedia.org/wiki/Pembroke_Welsh_Corgi#/me dia/File:Welchcorgipembroke.JPG>

Page 18 Photo By Flickr user Wplynn, <https://www.flickr. com/photos/warrenlynn/230449459/sizes/l>

Page 32 Photo By Dhlstrm via Wikimedia Commons, <https://commons.wikimedia.org/wiki/File:NordJW-06_Mudpaws_Duke_Silver.jpg>

Page 44 Photo By Lilly M via Wikimedia Commons, <https://commons.wikimedia.org/wiki/File:Welsh_Corgi_Pe

mbroke_Miedzynarodowa_wystawa_psow_rasowych_rybni
k_kamien_pazdziernik_2011_16.jpg>

Page 50 Photo By FatFairfax via Wikimedia Commons,
<https://en.wikipedia.org/wiki/Welsh_Corgi#/media/File:Car
digan_Welsh_Corgi,_Profile.png>

Page 62 Photo By Cmalaspina via Wikimedia Commons,
<https://en.wikipedia.org/wiki/Welsh_Corgi#/media/File:Cor
giRunning.jpg>

Page 70 Photo By Flickr user Melfr99, <https://www.flickr.
com/photos/33970504@N05/4244852774/sizes/l>

Page 77 Photo By Flickr user Evocateur, <https://www.flickr.
com/photos/evocateur/6365026845/sizes/l>

Page 86 Photo By Mbostock via Wikimedia Commons,
<https://commons.wikimedia.org/wiki/File:Pembroke_Corgi
_Image_001.jpg>

Page 93 Photo By FatFairfax via Wikimedia Commons,
<https://commons.wikimedia.org/wiki/File:Welsh_Corgi_Ca
rdigan_Licking.jpg>

Page 105 Photo By RdRnnr via Wikimedia Commons,
<https://commons.wikimedia.org/wiki/File:Cardigan_Welsh
_Corgi%27s.JPG>

References

"AAFCO Dog Food Nutrient Profiles." DogFoodAdvisor.
  <http://www.dogfoodadvisor.com/frequently-asked-
  questions/aafco-nutrient-profiles/>

"Annual Dog Care Costs." PetFinder.
  <https://www.petfinder.com/pet-adoption/dog-
  adoption/annual-dog-care-costs/>

"Canine Dental Disease." Banfield Pet Hospital.
  <http://www.banfield.com/pet-health-
  resources/preventive-care/dental/canine-dental-disease>

"Cardigan Welsh Corgi." AKC.org. <http://www.akc.org/
  dog-breeds/cardigan-welsh-corgi/>

"Cardigan Welsh Corgi." DogBreedInfo.com.
  <http://www.dogbreedinfo.com/cardigancorgi.htm

"Choosing a Healthy Puppy." WebMD.
  <http://pets.webmd.com/dogs/guide/choosing-healthy-
  puppy>

"Corgi Temperament." Corgi Guide. <http://corgiguide.com/
  corgi-temperament/>

"Grooming Tips for Corgis." The Nest Pets.
  <http://pets.thenest.com/grooming-tips-corgis-7709.html>

"How Much Do Corgis Cost." Corgi Guide.
  <http://corgiguide.com/how-much-corgis-cost/>

"How to Find a Responsible Breeder." HumaneSociety.org. <http://www.humanesociety.org/issues/puppy_mills/tips/finding_responsible_dog_breeder.html?referrer=https://www.google.com/>

"Is a Corgi Right for You?" The Corgi Site. <http://thecorgisite.com/index.php/want-a-corgi/is-a-corgi-right-for-you/>

"My Bowl: What Goes into a Balanced Diet for Your Dog?" PetMD. <http://www.petmd.com/dog/slideshows/nutrition-center/my-bowl-what-goes-into-a-balanced-diet-for-your-dog>

"Nutrients Your Dog Needs." ASPCA.org. <https://www.aspca.org/pet-care/dog-care/nutrients-your-dog-needs>

"Nutrition: General Feeding Guidelines for Dogs." VCA Animal Hospitals. <http://www.vcahospitals.com/main/pet-health-information/article/animal-health/nutrition-general-feeding-guidelines-for-dogs/6491>

"Official Standard of the Cardigan Welsh Corgi." AKC.org. <http://cdn.akc.org/CardiganWelshCorgi.pdf>

"Official Standard of the Pembroke Welsh Corgi." AKC.org. <http://cdn.akc.org/PembrokeWelshCorgi.pdf>

"Pembroke Welsh Corgi." AKC.org. <http://www.akc.org/dog-breeds/pembroke-welsh-corgi/>

"Pembroke Welsh Corgi." DogBreedInfo.com.
   <http://www.dogbreedinfo.com/pembrokecorgi.htm>

"Pembroke Welsh Corgi." DogTime.
   <http://dogtime.com/dog-breeds/pembroke-welsh-corgi

"Pembroke Welsh Corgis." K9 Web. <http://www.k9web.
   com/dog-faqs/breeds/pembrokes.html>

"Pet Care Costs." ASPCA.org. <https://www.aspca.org/
   adopt/pet-care-costs>

"Pros and Cons of the Welsh Corgi as a Good Pet for Your
   Family." The Daily Puppy. <http://dogcare.dailypuppy.
   com/pros-cons-welsh-corgi-good-pet-family-6926.html>

"Puppy Proofing Your Home." Hill's Pet.
   <http://www.hillspet.com/dog-care/puppy-proofing-your-
   home.html>

"Puppy Proofing Your Home." PetEducation.com.
   <http://www.peteducation.com/article.cfm?c=2+2106&aid=
   3283>

"Vitamins and Minerals Your Dog Needs." Kim Boatman.
   The Dog Daily. <http://www.thedogdaily.com/dish/diet/
   dogs_vitamins/index.html#.VHOtMPnF_IA>

Feeding Baby
Cynthia Cherry
978-1941070000

Axolotl
Lolly Brown
978-0989658430

Dysautonomia, POTS
Syndrome
Frederick Earlstein
978-0989658485

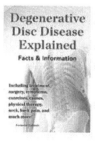

Degenerative Disc
Disease Explained
Frederick Earlstein
978-0989658485

Sinusitis, Hay Fever,
Allergic Rhinitis Explained
Frederick Earlstein
978-1941070024

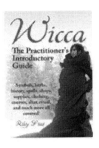

Wicca
Riley Star
978-1941070130

Zombie Apocalypse
Rex Cutty
978-1941070154

Capybara
Lolly Brown
978-1941070062

Eels As Pets
Lolly Brown
978-1941070167

Scabies and Lice Explained
Frederick Earlstein
978-1941070017

Saltwater Fish As Pets
Lolly Brown
978-0989658461

Torticollis Explained
Frederick Earlstein
978-1941070055

Kennel Cough
Lolly Brown
978-0989658409

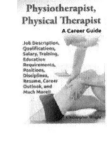

Physiotherapist, Physical
Therapist
Christopher Wright
978-0989658492

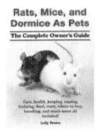

Rats, Mice, and Dormice
As Pets
Lolly Brown
978-1941070079

Wallaby and Wallaroo Care
Lolly Brown
978-1941070031

Bodybuilding Supplements
Explained
Jon Shelton
978-1941070239

Demonology
Riley Star
978-19401070314

Pigeon Racing
Lolly Brown
978-1941070307

Dwarf Hamster
Lolly Brown
978-1941070390

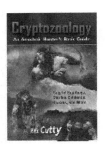

Cryptozoology
Rex Cutty
978-1941070406

Eye Strain
Frederick Earlstein
978-1941070369

Inez The Miniature Elephant
Asher Ray
978-1941070353

Vampire Apocalypse
Rex Cutty
978-1941070321